MANAGING STRESS

A PILGRIMAGE SMALL GROUP GUIDE
STEVE SHORES

NAVPRESS
BRINGING TRUTH TO LIFE
NavPress Publishing Group
P.O. Box 35001, Colorado Springs, Colorado 80935

The Navigators is an international Christian organization. Our mission is to reach, disciple, and equip people to know Christ and to make Him known through successive generations. We envision multitudes of diverse people in the United States and every other nation who have a passionate love for Christ, live a lifestyle of sharing Christ's love, and multiply spiritual laborers among those without Christ.

NavPress is the publishing ministry of The Navigators. NavPress publications help believers learn biblical truth and apply what they learn to their lives and ministries. Our mission is to stimulate spiritual formation among our readers.

ISBN 1-57683-083-7
Cover illustration by Randy Verougstraete/Stock Illustration Source

Some of the anecdotal illustrations in this book are true to life and are included with the permission of the persons involved. All other illustrations are composites of real situations, and any resemblance to people living or dead is coincidental.

Unless otherwise identified, all Scripture quotations in this publication are taken from the *HOLY BIBLE: NEW INTERNATIONAL VERSION* ® (NIV®). Copyright © 1973, 1978, 1984 by International Bible Society. Used by permission of Zondervan Publishing House. All rights reserved; and the *New American Standard Bible* (NASB), © The Lockman Foundation 1960, 1962, 1963, 1968, 1971, 1972, 1973, 1975, 1977.

Printed in the United States of America

1 2 3 4 5 6 7 8 9 10 11 12 13 14 15 / 01 00 99 98

Contents

How This Study Guide Works

It's considered normal today to be under pressure, in a hurry, juggling multiple responsibilities and wondering when the balls in the air will fly out of our control. Most people think such stress is caused by external factors: our boss's expectations, our kids' needs, our obligation to make a living.

Where is God in such a stressful world? Does the gospel have anything to say to people under stress who don't feel called to chuck it all and enter a monastery? In fact, is the gospel actually good news for people under pressure, or does it merely add another set of expectations to our already full calendars?

This study is designed to address questions like these in a small-group format. Participants will:

▶ engage in individual and group reflection
▶ participate in creative Bible study and group process
▶ learn to receive care from other group members
▶ pray together for God's work in each person's life

Building Community

The life of following Christ was never meant to be solitary. The early Christians pursued it in groups not much larger than your small group. They met exclusively in homes for the first two hundred years or so of the movement. By meeting in a small group, you are imitating a time-tested format for spiritual life.

People join small groups for all sorts of reasons: to get to know a few people well, to be cared for, to learn, to grow spiritually. We believe small groups are the ideal setting in which people can both learn what it means to take on the character of Christ and practice the process of becoming like Christ. While there are many spiritually helpful things one can do alone or in a large group, a small group offers many advantages. Among other things, group members can:

- ► encourage one another in good times and bad
- ► ask thoughtful questions when a member has a decision to make
- ► listen to God together
- ► learn how to pray
- ► pray for each other
- ► benefit from one another's insights into Scripture
- ► acquire a habit of reading the Bible on a regular basis
- ► practice loving their neighbors
- ► worship God together
- ► learn to communicate effectively
- ► solve problems together
- ► learn to receive care from others
- ► experience the pleasure of helping another person grow

This guide emphasizes learning and practice. It will help you to understand and do something about your stress in a non-threatening group environment. You will engage in reflection, study, interaction, and prayer. You will be challenged to put into practice what you are learning during the week.

A Modular Approach

Each session is divided into several modules or sections. Suggested times are allocated among the modules so that you can complete the session in 60 to 90 minutes. The primary modules include:

Overview: The first page of each session briefly describes the objectives for your meeting so that you will know what to expect during the meeting and what results to strive for. The overview also includes a story that sets the tone for the session.

Beginning: Building relationships is a necessary part of each group experience. The questions in this section will help you to get to know each other. They also will invite you to reflect on the overview story as a way of preparing for Bible study.

The Text: Studying a biblical text is an integral part of this guide. You will examine brief passages from various parts of the Bible. Because the New Testament was written to be read aloud, you will begin your study by reading the text aloud. Words in bold type are explained in the **Reference Notes** section.

Understanding the Text: Unless you notice carefully what the text says, you will not be able to interpret it accurately. The questions in this section will help you to focus on the key issues and wrestle with what the text means. In this section you will concentrate on the passage in its original first-century context.

Applying the Text: It is not enough simply to understand the passage; you need to apply that understanding to your situation. The questions in this section connect what you have read to how you intend to live.

Assignment: To allow for flexibility with how much time group members have to invest during the week, this guide offers homework as an elective. Your group may discuss the options found in each session as a means of continued growth and reflection. Make sure every group member agrees to do work before assigning it.

Prayer: Praying together can be one of the most faith-building and relationship-building things you do together. Suggestions are made to facilitate this time in the group.

Reference Notes: To understand accurately the meaning of the text, one needs to know a little about the context in which it was written and about the key words and phrases it contains. The notes include background on the characters, information about cultural practices, word definitions, and so on. You will find entries in this section for those words and phrases in the text that are printed in bold type. You can scan the notes after reading the text aloud, or during your discussion of Understanding the Text.

Additional Resources: A list of books that address the session's topic will end some sessions.

Help for the Leader

This Growth Guide provides everything the leader needs to facilitate the group's discussion. In each session, the symbol ❶ designates instructions for the leader.

Answers to Common Questions

Who is this material designed for?

▶ Anyone who wants to learn about the causes of stress and what we can do about it.

▶ Ongoing groups that want to support each other in addressing the stress in members' lives.

How often should we meet?

▶ Once a week is best; every other week also works well.

How long should we meet?

▶ You will need at least an hour.
▶ Ninety minutes is best—this gives time for more discussion.
▶ Some groups may want to meet for two hours, especially if you have more than eight people.

What if we only have 50 minutes?

▶ Cut back on the **Beginning** section and choose just one question under **Applying the Text**. Pray only briefly.

Is homework necessary?

▶ No, the group can meet with no prior preparation.
▶ The assignments will greatly increase what you gain from the group.

Session One

How Life Got to Be So Stressful

▼ ▼ ▼ ▼ ▼ ▼ ▼ ▼ ▼ ▼ ▼ ▼ ▼ ▼ ▼ ▼ ▼ ▼ ▼ ▼

Overview   10 minutes

❶ *Make sure everybody has been welcomed to the group
and the room is comfortably arranged. If group members don't
know one another, exchange names. If they don't know you,
introduce yourself to the group, sharing:*

- ▶ your name
- ▶ your leadership role in the group
- ▶ several objectives you have for this group

*Then, briefly share your agenda for the meeting. What do you
want to happen? What do you want the group to get out of the
session? Make sure everyone has a copy of this study guide, then
have someone read the following story and session objectives:*

On the morning of writing this chapter, I drove to a city about sev-
enty miles away and sat through a continuing education seminar.
It was great. I loved it. Not because of the content, but because I
could just sit back, take a few notes, and soak in the results of
someone else's labor. I was like a tea bag in reverse, being infused
with the benefits of another's toil. Halfway through the seminar,
the teacher announced that she wanted us to divide into small
groups to analyze a case study. I tensed up. Why? My soaking was
over. Now I had to get with a group of strangers and figure out

how to handle this counseling case. Ugh! Back to work. It felt like what I'd been doing all week: pulling too much weight.

In this session we'll talk about

▶ how the weight—the stress of life—got to be there in the first place
▶ how stress, within limits, can be good
▶ the message in our stress

▼ ▼ ▼ ▼ ▼ ▼ ▼ ▼ ▼ ▼ ▼ ▼ ▼ ▼ ▼ ▼ ▼ ▼ ▼ ▼

Beginning   15 minutes

➊ *Have everyone read this poem silently.*

A Psalm While Packing Books

This cardboard box
Lord
see it says
Bursting limit
200 lbs. per square inch
The box maker knew
how much strain
the box would take
what weight
would crush it.
You are wiser
than the box maker
Maker of my spirit
my mind
my body.
Does the box know
when pressure increases close to
the limit?
No
it knows nothing.
But I know

when my breaking point
is near.
And so I pray
Maker of my soul
Determiner of the pressure
within
upon
me
Stop it
lest I be broken
or else
change the pressure rating
of this fragile container
of Your grace
so that I may bear more.[1]

We can relate to the idea of having a bursting limit, a pressure rating that seems inadequate for the load that life dumps on us. Most of us would agree that our boxes are overfilled and strained to the bursting point. So what do we do? Dump everything out of the box and walk away?

By sharing our stories with one another, we'll be able to pool our thoughts about how life gets so stressful. We also can learn how to affect one another's lives for the good.

❶ *Go around the room and allow each person to answer the first question before moving to the next one. The leader should answer first each time.*

1. In your experience, how has stress been bad for you? What do you see as your major causes of stress?

   ❏ finances
   ❏ children
   ❏ marriage
   ❏ job
   ❏ in-laws or extended family
   ❏ guilt or frustration from a past failure
   ❏ shortage of time
   ❏ church
   ❏ other:

2. If you could change one thing in your life to make it less stressful, what would it be?

▼ ▼
The Text   5 minutes

The Gospel of Matthew presents Jesus as the great King, the One
who rules in every sphere and over every power. He rebukes a
storm, and it quiets like a chastened child. He commands the
demons, and they flee, crying out in terror. He calls a leper to
wholeness, and the man's body responds to the One who made it.
      But the powerful King is also a wise King. This is the focus of
the Sermon on the Mount (Matthew 5–7). Jesus' teaching is like a
spearhead of the kingdom of God, thrusting forward, probing and
restoring the minds of men and women. But not all minds are
ready. Only those who are willing to become like children can hear
this wise King's teaching, so a few chapters later He says, "I praise
you, Father, Lord of heaven and earth, because you have hidden
these things from the wise and learned, and revealed them to little
children" (Matthew 11:25). What does Jesus mean by "little children"? In our text for this session, He gives us the major character
quality of the kind of "child" for whom He is looking.

❶ *Have someone read the text aloud. You may also read any
or all of the reference notes on pages 18-19.*

Come to me, all you who are **weary and burdened**, and I will give
you rest. Take my yoke upon you and learn from me, for I am
gentle and humble, and you will find rest for your souls. For my
yoke is easy and my burden is light.

(Matthew 11:28-30)

12

Understanding the Text   20 minutes

3. a. When Jesus says, "Come to me," what do you think that
      might look like?

   b. Describe some ways you have come to Him. Which ways
      have been more effective, and which have been less so?

Millie has been a Christian for a long time. Lately, she has
had to admit that unless she stays super busy, she feels unquiet
inside. There's an agitation that underlies the busy schedule that
has always served to distract her. When she first mentions this to a
Christian friend, she is advised to pray about it. The friend, too,
promises to pray. After a month of this, Millie feels the agitation is,
if anything, worse. She tells this to her friend, who is sympathetic,
puzzled, and says, "Maybe you should see a counselor." Millie feels
superficially dealt with by her friend. It's not that she's against seeing a counselor, but she thought this friend would engage more
deeply with her struggle.

4. a. Millie isn't experiencing the rest Christ offers. How would you
      evaluate the advice Millie's friend gives her?

   b. How would you have wanted Millie's friend to approach her?

Suppose Millie goes to a counselor and learns that her
assertiveness skills are lacking. She works on those skills diligently.

13

She says "no" more. She becomes less busy. But she still senses that restlessness inside. The counselor thinks the restlessness stems from pain rooted in the extreme criticism Millie experienced in childhood. They work on her self-image.

5. In the text for this session, Jesus says, "Take my yoke upon you." How might Millie's attempt to apply Jesus' words look different from her attempts to bolster her self-image and assertiveness?

6. Let's say another of Millie's friends recommends spending more time in the Bible, rather than in counseling. When Jesus says, "Learn of me," is He asking for more in-depth Bible study? What might He be offering that cannot be gained by focusing on Bible study skills alone?

7. How do you feel when you're in pain and you receive advice like that given to Millie (such as "Pray more" or "Go to a counselor")? Try to express what you want when you're in pain. Why doesn't such advice usually touch that pain?

I make my living as a counselor, so obviously I'm not opposed to counseling. However, I think some people go to counselors for things they might be better off getting from a deep, committed community, if such a place is available. And other people who do need counseling also need this same kind of community.

8. How could a community of people deeply committed to each other help Millie? What qualities of such a community could help her?

❶ *Have someone (or several people taking turns) read the following essay aloud.*

Someone might say, "It's easy to figure out why I'm stressed. I'm stressed because I'm so busy! Travel time alone amounts to at least an hour-and a-half per day for me. What's the mystery?" In other words, our stress is due to external factors. But what gives those external factors their ability to snare us? Why are they so hard to resist? Why does a mother have to crisscross a city six times in one day to accommodate soccer practices? Do her children really want to do this? Or have they detected an urging in her (or her husband) to which they're responding? Maybe her lifestyle is more the result of choice than she is willing to admit. Maybe there are internal factors to take into account. What might they be?

Stress will be defined in this study as anything that pushes us away from equilibrium. Equilibrium describes those times when we are completely comfortable and tension-free in any area: physical, emotional, social, or spiritual. All creatures seek equilibrium, and it's tempting to say the human creature should learn from other creatures (from bacteria to chimps) and make equilibrium the goal of life.

While I *do* want the vital organs in my body to seek equilibrium (I want my heart, for example, to stay in a certain comfort zone), it's less simple to say the human *soul* ought to seek such balance in this world. The arresting truth is that our souls are not built for this world because it's fallen. Because of the intrusion of sin, the world has deteriorated. Once a paradise for the human body and soul, it is now inhospitable to both. Being strangers and aliens here, we long for a new paradise that has been offered but not yet delivered. Our souls, then, are automatically pushed far from the equilibrium that will be ours in heaven. A fallen world tears at us, makes it a strain just to live life. We are no more designed for this world than a cotton ball is designed for a carwash.

This means there will, in this world, always be something amiss inside us. Something within is out of joint. The disjointedness is there because we're not yet at home with God. Quite simply, we're homesick. Our homesickness has a message: that we're decidedly *not* home, but that God has come looking for us. This means that, should we seek comfort anywhere else, we'll not find it. That's why Jesus says, "Come to me." Jesus summons us to Himself, because intimacy with Him is the answer to the strain of living here.

This summons has both vertical and horizontal dimensions. The *vertical dimension* has to do with an everyday Christianity centered on practicing the presence of Christ with the help of the Holy Spirit—what Jesus refers to when He says, "Abide in Me" (John 15:4, NASB). The *horizontal dimension* involves a deeper connection with other Christians, one that brings true fellowship and intimate engagement with one another. Notice that both the vertical and the horizontal pivot on connection. For most of us, our connection, both with Christ and with our brothers and sisters, is anemic. Much of our stress stems from seeking to live without the benefit of vital connectedness. We're like a runner at high altitude, faltering because the air is so thin. Both vertical and horizontal connectedness will be developed in this study.

Applying the Text   20 minutes

9. Remember Millie? Having read the preceding essay, what would you say underlies that restlessness she feels?

10. The essay describes our being homesick for heaven. Have you ever experienced that?

11. a. When Jesus calls out to the "weary and burdened," in what ways is He talking to you?

   b. In what different way might He want you to come to Him in a different way than you've approached Him before?

12. Do you think your connectedness with other believers is anemic? If so, what factors might be contributing to your lack of connectedness?

▼ ▼ ▼ ▼ ▼ ▼ ▼ ▼ ▼ ▼ ▼ ▼ ▼ ▼ ▼ ▼ ▼ ▼ ▼ ▼
Assignment   10 minutes

Decide which of the following homework electives you will do. Your whole group may decide to do the same elective or simply let each member pick.

   Elective 1: Reflection—Reflect on the following questions in your journal this week: Would you agree that people in our culture have a love affair with personal comfort? Why would you say that? Would you say that you, too, have had a love affair with comfort? Is it wrong to be comfortable? Where does a concern with being comfortable become imbalanced? What would you say are some of the sources of our love affair with comfort?

Elective 2: Project—Take some time to think about the aspects of your life that make you ache inside. This may be hard to do, because most of us feel pressure to stay upbeat, especially as Christians. If you can, give yourself permission to think honestly about the ache. You might title a sheet of paper, "Things in My Life that Make Me Ache," then list as many sources of ache as you can think of. Talk candidly with God about your list: "Here's my list, God. It's quite a load, and I feel exhausted. Please give me the faith and endurance I need to walk with You." Pray along these lines, then record in your journal what you feel God is showing you.

▼ ▼
Prayer   5 minutes

Allow each person to answer this question:

How familiar am I with the ache inside?

- ❏ intimately familiar
- ❏ familiar with it from time to time
- ❏ I understand the concept but don't feel the ache
- ❏ I don't grasp the concept very well

Let the various responses be turned into sentence prayers for one another. No response should be judged. The point is to lift one another to the Lord, no matter what the response.

▼ ▼ ▼ ▼ ▼ ▼ ▼ ▼ ▼ ▼ ▼ ▼ ▼ ▼ ▼ ▼ ▼ ▼
Reference Notes

Setting: Matthew presents Jesus as the King who rules in every sphere. In chapters 11 and 12, Israel repudiates her King decisively, despite His demonstrations of power and miracles in every sphere of life.[2] Israel reveals that her blindness is both complete and self-chosen. Jesus, in turn, begins to focus on offering His kingdom to His disciples. He turns away from the sinful heart of Israel, a heart that insists on continuing to labor and becoming weary in prideful self-effort. Jesus turns to those who want to cease their labors, admitting that those labors spring from self-sufficiency. To these He says, "Come to me, all who are weary and burdened, and I will give you rest."

weary and burdened: The root idea in the word "weary" is that of being beaten or struck. Behind the word "burdened" is a Greek term that refers to cargo, especially that on a ship. Jesus could be paraphrased as saying, "Come to Me, all you whom life has given a beating, all you who are sinking in life like an overloaded ship."

gentle and humble: "Gentle" refers to a spirit that does not contend with God, one that instead accepts His dealings with us— because we are convinced that He is good—without disputing or resisting them. This does not mean we can't be honest with God, but that, in the end, God will be vindicated in His sovereignty; and we accept that in spite of our confusion. Jesus exemplifies this spirit in His acceptance of God's mission for Him (see Philippians 2:5-8). "Humble" has to do with being low, the opposite of exalted. For Christ, this meant a confession of absolute dependence on His Father. This is the same dependence to which He invites us when He says, "Take my yoke upon you."

yoke: The idea is to be joined and thus to go in the same direction. Christ says that being yoked with Him is a joining that is easy and light. This is something we must come to know over time. Thus, he says, "Learn of Me." It's a process. As we learn of Him, we learn of His dependence on His Father and are invited more and more deeply into it.

▼ ▼ ▼ ▼ ▼ ▼ ▼ ▼ ▼ ▼ ▼ ▼ ▼ ▼ ▼ ▼ ▼ ▼

Additional Resources

Alcorn, Randy and Nanci. *Women Under Stress*. Portland, OR: Multnomah, 1986.

Friedman, Meyer and Ray H. Rosenman. *Type A Behavior and Your Heart*. New York: Knopf, 1974.

Hart, Archibald. *Adrenaline and Stress*, rev. ed. Dallas: Word, 1995.
Tournier, Paul, ed. *Fatigue and Modern Society*. Richmond, VA: John Knox Press, 1965.

▼ ▼ ▼ ▼ ▼ ▼ ▼ ▼ ▼ ▼ ▼ ▼ ▼ ▼ ▼ ▼ ▼ ▼

Food for Thought

Jesus' "human life was a constant living on the fullness of his Father's love."

—Richard Trench,
Synonyms of the New Testament
(Grand Rapids, Mich.: Eerdmans, 1953)

---

1. Joseph Bayly, cited in Randy and Nanci Alcorn, *Women Under Stress* (Portland, Ore: Multnomah, 1986), p. 26.
2. See "Matthew, the Gospel According to," *The Oxford Companion to the Bible* (Oxford: Oxford University Press, 1993), p. 504.

Session Two

Loathing Our Limits

▼ ▼ ▼ ▼ ▼ ▼ ▼ ▼ ▼ ▼ ▼ ▼ ▼ ▼ ▼ ▼ ▼ ▼ ▼

Overview   10 minutes

🄻 *Make sure any newcomers are introduced and given the appropriate materials. Exchange names if group members' memories need to be refreshed.*

Allow group members to share what they learned from their homework. Also, encourage members to recap what they learned from the last session. Then ask someone to read aloud this story and the objectives that follow.

It's snowing. That means I have time to write this chapter. But the *reason* I have all this time is because my counselees for today are snowed in. This means (1) I have no income for today (and probably much of tomorrow because it's still snowing late in the afternoon); and (2) I'm feeling pressure to make a bunch of phone calls and somehow reschedule everyone I didn't see today. The message I'm hearing in my head is, "It's completely up to you to generate the income for this family. Do you think typing into a computer is going to refill your appointment book? Your family is going to be hurt by this. If you were aggressive enough, creative enough, ingenious enough, your family wouldn't have to worry. But because you're you, they're going to be let down." Getting out from under stress involves combating messages exactly like these. In this session we will learn:

- ► how we increase our stress by fighting hard to be "enough"
- ► why we loathe our limits
- ► how depending on God will help us accept our limits and lower our stress

▼ ▼ ▼ ▼ ▼ ▼ ▼ ▼ ▼ ▼ ▼ ▼ ▼ ▼ ▼ ▼ ▼ ▼ ▼

Beginning   20 minutes

❶ *Go around the room and allow each person to answer the first question before moving to the next one. The leader should answer first each time.*

1. Do you identify with those internal messages from the Overview story? Share a message you hear from time to time that raises your stress level.

2. a. The word "enough" occurs three times in the story. What have you done in your own life to be "enough"?

    b. How have you responded when you've concluded, for whatever reasons, you can't be "enough" for a given situation?
       ❏ I had an outburst of anger.
       ❏ I dipped into depression for a time.
       ❏ I blamed someone else for my inadequacy.
       ❏ I became extremely critical of others.
       ❏ I withdrew from everyone.
       ❏ Other:

3. Pressure to be "enough" often translates into a fear and hatred of our limits. (After all, what is the drive to be "enough" if not a push to transcend our limits?) What limitation(s) have you struggled with?

❑ I've always thought I wasn't smart enough.
❑ I've struggled with feeling I'm not attractive enough.
❑ I'm too short.
❑ I'm too tall.
❑ I can't think well on my feet; I wish I were mentally quicker.
❑ I have this feeling I'll never measure up.
❑ I wish I weren't so awkward in social situations.
❑ I don't think I'm tough enough; I'm afraid I come across as weak.
❑ I have a physical limitation that others seem impatient with at times.
❑ Other:

▼ ▼ ▼ ▼ ▼ ▼ ▼ ▼ ▼ ▼ ▼ ▼ ▼ ▼ ▼ ▼ ▼ ▼

The Text   5 minutes

In Genesis 32, Jacob is nearing the end of his career as a major manipulator. Through conniving and cunning, he has bested his father Isaac and his brother Esau, and has manipulated his uncle Laban to a draw. Now he is facing his day of reckoning with Esau, and he knows he could lose everything. He remains awake all night, wrestling a foe he can't sneak up on: God Himself!

So Jacob was left alone, and **a man** wrestled with him till daybreak. When the man saw that he could not overpower him, he touched the socket of Jacob's hip so that **his hip was wrenched** as he wrestled with the man. Then the man said, "Let me go, for it is daybreak."

But Jacob replied, "I will not let you go unless you bless me."
The man asked him, "What is your name?"

23

"Jacob," he answered.

Then the man said, "Your name will no longer be **Jacob**, but **Israel**, because you have struggled with God and with men and have overcome."

Jacob said, "Please tell me your name."

But he replied, "Why do you ask my name?" Then he blessed him there.

So Jacob called the place Peniel, saying, "It is because I saw God face to face, and yet my life was spared."

The sun rose above him as he passed Peniel, and he was limping because of his hip.

(Genesis 32:24-31)

▼ ▼ ▼ ▼ ▼ ▼ ▼ ▼ ▼ ▼ ▼ ▼ ▼ ▼ ▼ ▼ ▼ ▼
Understanding the Text   15 minutes

Jacob clings tenaciously to God and will not let go until God blesses him. This muscular clinging adds a level of complexity to the scene we studied in session 1 from Matthew 11:28-30. There Jesus invites us to crawl into God's lap to rest. Here, Jacob is cinched tightly around God's torso, holding firmly to God no matter what threatens to tear him away. In the Matthew passage we are told to turn from our self-sufficiency. Here we have an example of a man who exerts every effort to hold onto God in spite of pressure to give up and let go.

4. What picture of depending on God does this text present?

5. What are Jacob's limitations in this story?

24

When God saw that "he could not overpower him [Jacob],"
God "touched the socket of Jacob's hip so that his hip was
wrenched." Given God's power over Jacob in the second half of
the sentence, the first half is probably a tongue-in-cheek way of
saying that God had not yet begun to exert His real power.

6. a. After God shows His true power, what are Jacob's next words?

    b. What do these words imply about gaining God's blessing?

▼ ▼ ▼ ▼ ▼ ▼ ▼ ▼ ▼ ▼ ▼ ▼ ▼ ▼ ▼ ▼ ▼
Applying the Text   20 minutes

7. After twenty years of relying on his own wits to make his way in
   the world, Jacob is finally backed into such a corner that he has
   no alternative but to wrestle alone with God and hang on until
   God blesses him. Where are you in this process?

   ❑ I'm still doing fine at making my way by my own wits.
   ❑ I feel like my own efforts aren't enough, but I'm not to
      the point of wrestling alone with God.
   ❑ I'm wrestling with God, but it seems to be taking an
      awfully long time.
   ❑ I feel like God has wrenched my hip, but I'm trying to
      hang on.
   ❑ I have received God's blessing, but I still walk with a limp.
   ❑ I don't see myself anywhere in this story.

From Genesis 32 we can discern several principles:

- ▶ When we approach life in combat mode (as Jacob did), God may wrestle with us.
- ▶ Some of the wear and tear we feel in life *may* stem from the fact that God is wisely opposing us to show us our limits.
- ▶ Jacob only prevailed when he saw that he *couldn't* prevail. That is, we win when we lose to God, allowing Him to teach us how much we need Him.
- ▶ God wants us to "walk with a limp"—to accept those limitations we can't change.

8. Thinking of the above principles, read the following situation and discuss how someone who is working to accept limits might respond.

> Jerry never got his father's approval. No matter how hard he worked, tried, performed, excelled, his father always found a way to say, "You could've done better." Jerry can't relax about this. He's still trying to get his father to say, "Attaboy!" Now, anyone who tries to be honest with him risks triggering his rage. Any criticism now taps into the hurt and anger Jerry feels toward his father.

a. How is Jerry increasing his stress by trying to be "enough"?

b. What would he have to accept in order to stop trying?

c. What limit, then, would Jerry have to live with? Describe this in terms of Jerry walking with a limp.

d. How might Jerry need to turn to God for the blessing his father never gave?

When we seek God's blessing as tenaciously as Jacob did, we may have to forgo whatever blessings we think might accrue from being "enough." For instance, we may have to sacrifice the blessings that would come from working eighty-hour weeks and involving our kids in all the best programs. It might be that our stress level will fluctuate to the degree that we accept our limits and agree that the benefits of following Christ are worth the costs.

9. How do you feel about the idea that the peace of God might involve accepting both limits and costs?

❶ *Have someone (or several people taking turns) read the following essay aloud.*

When I read Jesus' summons from Matthew 11, "Come to me, all who are weary and loaded down," I feel a twinge of frustration. Why? Because His summons reminds me that I'm limited, and I don't like to admit that. My limits diminish me, and there's a part of me that broods about it. I feel I've got to keep up! I don't want it to look as though I can't do what everybody else does. Not only do I have to "keep up with the Joneses" materially, but also in my level of activity, in my trying to do more and more in less and less time. Then you throw in the "Christian Joneses." How many Bible studies are enough? How many outreach activities? How many holiday events? How many youth concerts? How many retreats? How many work days? How many committee meetings? How much visitation?

27

We loathe our limits because we don't want to lag behind. But have we thought this through? The people with whom we are trying desperately to keep up, where are *they* going? It's obvious they are in a hurry, but toward what? To answer that question, and to see why we hate our limits, we have to think about two recent revolutions: the Individualist Revolution and the Industrial Revolution.

The Individualist Revolution has its roots in the seventeenth- and eighteenth-century Enlightenment, a period in which human reason took center stage from faith. With reason on the throne, the individual and his ability to think for himself gradually replaced a more communal lifestyle that drew from rich sources of faith and tradition. As these latter two fell away, the individual was left more and more free, yet more and more isolated. Self replaced God as the center of life. This process was accelerated by the nineteenth-century Romantic movement, which essentially elevated feeling even above reason. Thus, how I *feel*, even more than how I think, came to be central. Finally, the humanistic psychology of the mid- to late-twentieth century completed the Individualist Revolution. This psychology, especially as developed by Abraham Maslow, described self-actualization (reaching my fullest potential) as the pinnacle of life. Western culture is utterly "dedicated to the actualized self,"[1] and this dedication is even higher in America than in Europe. (That the self is something you'd want to actualize is a bit harder to swallow when two world wars have been fought under your nose.) What are Americans hurrying after? Much of it revolves around the full development of self, both for themselves and their children.

If Enlightenment + Romantic movement + Maslow makes us into narcissists, the Industrial Revolution converts us into machines. We become used to producing, to generating measurable outputs that contribute to our value. This compulsive production mindset makes it hard for us to cultivate a deep connection with God (the vertical dimension we discussed in chapter one) and others (the horizontal dimension). We are too busy in our machinelike lives to connect deeply with anyone.

The combined effect of these two revolutions? Narcissistic machines! In other words, to the degree we have imbibed the values of our culture, we tend compulsively to generate the behaviors that will actualize the unconnected self. We are marked, then, by two features: time urgency and lack of community (both vertical and horizontal). We are filled with hurry-sickness and are hurled forward in isolation.

We hate our limits, then, because they suggest that our hurry is fruitless (no matter how hard we try, we can never reach that self-satisfying pinnacle) and that we need others, especially

God. Our limits tell us that we're needy, but narcissists are afraid of needs, and machines aren't supposed to have any.

Assignment   5 minutes

Elective 1: Essay—Take some time to write in your journal about the preceding essay. To what extent are you driven by the belief that your purpose in life is to produce as much as possible (you are a machine)? To what extent are you driven by the belief that you must make sure you and your children achieve your fullest potential?

Elective 2: Reflection—Complete the following sentence with the personal limitations you seek to conceal from others. Reflect on how you have increased your stress by refusing to accept those limits that can't be changed. "If people really knew this about me, they would avoid me because . . ."

Prayer   5 minutes

With the leader going first, have each person pray (either aloud or silently) about a limitation he or she would like to work on accepting.

Reference Notes

Setting: As a young man, Jacob cheated his brother Esau, then fled when Esau was planning to kill him. He spent twenty years working for his uncle, then had to flee from there when tensions between him and his uncle peaked. Now in middle age, Jacob decides he must quit running and face his brother. As he nears Esau's home, though, he receives word that Esau is approaching with four hundred armed men. Jacob knows his brother may kill him tomorrow, but he is determined to face the music, so he sends his family and employees off to safety and spends the night alone with God.

a man: The end of the story indicates that this man was somehow God.

his hip was wrenched: God put Jacob's hip out of joint with a mere touch. Since that joint is so strategic to wrestling, the match was essentially over at that point.

Jacob . . . Israel: The name "Jacob" means "schemer" and refers to his nature as a manipulator and cheat. "Israel" means "God fights" or "he fights with God." Two important things emerge from this change of name: (1) the superior always names the inferior in Scripture, so this is the second sign of God's power over Jacob (the first being the dislocating of his hip); (2) Jacob's nature has now been broken and then changed for the better. Rather than scheming and plotting, Jacob/Israel will now rely on a God, who fought with him in order to fight *for* him.

▼ ▼ ▼ ▼ ▼ ▼ ▼ ▼ ▼ ▼ ▼ ▼ ▼ ▼ ▼ ▼ ▼ ▼ ▼
Additional Resources

Foster, Richard J. *The Freedom of Simplicity*. San Francisco: HarperSanFrancisco, 1981.

Viorst, Judith. *Necessary Losses*. New York: Ballantine Books, 1986.

---

1. "Roe: Twenty-Five Years Later," *First Things* (January 1998, Number 79), p. 9.

Session Three

How Pursuing Approval Makes Stress Explosive

▼ ▼ ▼ ▼ ▼ ▼ ▼ ▼ ▼ ▼ ▼ ▼ ▼ ▼ ▼ ▼ ▼ ▼ ▼ ▼

Overview   10 minutes

❶ *Allow group members to share what they learned from their homework. Also, encourage people to recap what they learned from last session. Then ask someone to read aloud this story and the objectives that follow.*

Some years ago, my wife and I had guests over for dinner. My oldest daughter brought out a school fundraising project for our friends to consider. My daughter was shy about speaking up, and I found myself prompting her. "Why don't you just read it to them?" I said with a plastic smile that was stiffening into anguish. My thoughts were something like this: "My daughter is going to look like a buffoon in front of our friends (who have, incidentally, incredibly articulate children), and I'll be implicated. An inarticulate kid can only come from an inadequate father, right?" In my conflict with my own fears, I completely lost sight of my daughter's well-being.

In this session we'll explore:

► how we multiply our stress by an inordinate desire for approval
► how gaining approval often means remaining hidden from others
► how we'd rather risk exhaustion than be discovered
► how to begin detaching from an overemphasis on approval

▼ ▼ ▼ ▼ ▼ ▼ ▼ ▼ ▼ ▼ ▼ ▼ ▼ ▼ ▼ ▼ ▼ ▼ ▼
Beginning   10 minutes

1. In the story above, the visiting friends have "incredibly articulate children." How does that increase the father's internal conflict?

2. When the father prompts his daughter ("Why don't you just read it to them?"), what is his motive?

3. How does selfishness heighten the father's stress level?

The Text   5 minutes

❶ *Have someone read the following text.*

Genesis 2–3 recounts the story of the first humans, Adam and Eve.
The following two verses bracket the famous incident in which the
couple eats fruit from the tree of the knowledge of good and evil:

The man and his wife were both **naked**, and they felt no **shame**.
(Genesis 2:25)

Then the eyes of both of them were opened, and they realized they
were naked; so they sewed fig leaves together and made **coverings**
for themselves.
(Genesis 3:7)

Understanding the Text   10 minutes

4. How does the couple's disobedience change them? How are
   they different in the second verse?

5. What was the point of the fig leaves? Why did the people sud-
   denly feel the need to cover their nakedness?

33

6. Read the Reference Notes on page 39. How would you explain what shame means from a biblical point of view?

▼ ▼ ▼ ▼ ▼ ▼ ▼ ▼ ▼ ▼ ▼ ▼ ▼ ▼ ▼ ▼ ▼ ▼
Applying the Text   25 minutes

7. For Adam and Eve, openness gave way to hiding, or covering up. What influences Christians to hide from one another?

8. Shame is the fear that we will be hurt (rejected, devalued) if something about us is exposed. How did the father in our opening story display shame?

9. Shame leads us to hide, cover up, withdraw. In what ways, if any, do you hide or withdraw from people?

   ❏ I keep a stiff, distant stance in most relationships.
   ❏ I work hard to keep the emotional temperature down; I am the "thermostat" who takes on the anxious role of minimizing conflict.
   ❏ I work harder to be inoffensive than to be honest.
   ❏ I rarely make eye contact with others.

❏ I use an automatic, social smile for most occasions.
❏ I wear a stoic, nonexpressive mask that reveals little of
   what I'm feeling.
❏ I live out a controllable, well-rehearsed role (like being a
   "good Christian").
❏ I strive for such things as achievements, recognition, or
   diplomas behind which to screen myself.
❏ I don't think I do anything to hide or withdraw.
❏ Other:

10. How might withdrawing from others reflect a failure to trust
    God and a determination to be in control of our lives?

11. How might a habit of interpersonal withdrawal contribute to
    heightened stress?

12. Take a moment on your own to fill in the following sentence.
    (Share your answer if you feel comfortable doing so with this
    group.) "If people really knew this about me, they would reject
    or ridicule me because . . ."

13. How might working hard to prevent people from knowing this
    lead to increased stress?

14. What, if anything, do you do to seek approval that hurts either yourself or others?

☐ I spend excessive time on my personal appearance.
☐ I make sure the house is perfect when company is coming.
☐ I squelch what I really think because I sense the other person would disapprove, even though it's my honest opinion.
☐ I edit what I say so that it comes out "just right."
☐ I push my kids to achieve.
☐ I have to own the right car, clothes, toys, et cetera.
☐ I don't know of anything I do to seek approval that hurts anyone.
☐ Other:

❶ *Have one or two people read the following essay aloud.*

Let's go back to my embarrassment over my daughter's shyness. My insecurity led me to scramble for some fig leaves to cover my inadequacies as a parent. Maybe I could prompt her without being too obvious. Or maybe I could use humor to take the attention off her. Maybe I could take over, make the presentation (at least partly) myself.

Notice that none of these maneuvers give me any real control. What if my prompting becomes too transparent? What if my humor falls flat? What if I take over and hurt my daughter in the process?

Managing shame is impossible! I'll never have enough fig leaves. Or the ones I have will fall off. Or they'll be so obvious that everyone will know I'm hiding.

All attempts to cover shame are inadequate. But in my foolishness I respond by working harder than ever at creating fig leaves. I'm too afraid to think about stopping the whole process. I'd rather risk exhaustion than exposure.

Why is it so painful to be exposed, to be seen to the core? Ask my daughter. Depending on how blatantly I intervened, she may well have gone away from that scene feeling humiliated. She may have thought, "When I do something in front of Dad, I must do it perfectly or not at all. I guess he assumes I'll fail. He probably can't

count on me to make him look good. I wish I could do better."
One outcome, notice, is that she begins to question herself, not
because *she's* truly inadequate, but because *I* feel inadequate. Her
temptation is to conclude that she's a substandard human being,
sort of a semi-human. If that's true, it must never be discovered!
Thus, life becomes a frantic effort to feel acceptable and not let
others down.

Early messages of uselessness, then, lead to a life of internal
self-condemnation. But why would anyone live that way, in such a
mire of self-accusation? This may not seem obvious at first, but
self-condemnation is actually an effective anesthetic. It numbs the
soul! The pain of self-condemnation numbs a greater pain, that of
understanding our wounds and seeing that those who shamed us
acted in truly harmful ways. How much would my daughter really
want to see the evil in how I distanced myself from her?

We have looked, in this session, at several factors that
increase stress. First we saw how *selfishness* boosts stress. Then
we explored how *interpersonal withdrawal*—working hard to
cover up—multiplies stress. While we keep our internal world
hidden, we make an intense effort outwardly to *strive for
approval.* Thus, we have the stress of repressing parts of who we
really are while developing a sham persona impressive enough to
lure others into affirming us. While this outward show goes on,
the secret of who we really are distresses us, so we work even
harder to create "fig leaves." Our *shame* drives this hiding and
adds to our stress. We then deprecate ourselves (*self-condemnation*), believing that others will not shame someone who is already
ashamed of himself.

We might say, then, that much of our stress comes from
withdrawing our truer selves from others while extending a false
self that probes for approval. We are stressed because we don't
truly connect with one another. The quest for approval involves a
journey away from community.

15. How does habitual self-condemnation (otherwise known as
    low self-esteem) increase one's level of stress?

▼ ▼ ▼ ▼ ▼ ▼ ▼ ▼ ▼ ▼ ▼ ▼ ▼ ▼ ▼ ▼ ▼ ▼ ▼ ▼
Assignment   5 minutes

Elective 1: Bible Study—Read Psalm 32:5-7, and reflect on the following questions:

- ▶ Notice the relief David felt when he allowed his sin to be exposed. Have you ever experienced a similar relief from allowing exposure (whether of sinful or nonsinful things) to come? Jot down your thoughts about why this felt relieving.
- ▶ Take a few moments to contemplate your life. Is there any area in which you think you should let exposure come, rather than working hard to prevent it? Write that area down and be prepared to share it with the group.
- ▶ Read Psalm 32:1-2. Why is it "blessed" to have one's sin forgiven? Why is this so much better than carrying deep shame?

Elective 2: Reflection—Recall my reaction to my daughter's shyness. At one point I completely lost sight of her well-being because of my own fear. This week, take a blank sheet of paper and consider whether you've ever been in my daughter's shoes. When have you experienced someone else forgetting about your well-being because of his or her own fears? Write down a few sentences about the experience, especially about *how you felt* and *what you did in reaction to the experience.* Be prepared to share with the group.

▼ ▼ ▼ ▼ ▼ ▼ ▼ ▼ ▼ ▼ ▼ ▼ ▼ ▼ ▼ ▼ ▼ ▼ ▼ ▼
Prayer   5 minutes

With the leader going first, have each person pray (either aloud or silently) to be freed from worrying about approval and freed to extend the love of Christ in real connection with others.

▼ ▼ ▼ ▼ ▼ ▼ ▼ ▼ ▼ ▼ ▼ ▼ ▼ ▼ ▼ ▼ ▼ ▼ ▼

Reference Notes

Setting: Before disobeying God, Adam and Eve lived together naked (not just physically, but also interpersonally) and unashamed. However, sin brought with it:

- ► new awareness ("the eyes of both of them were opened")
- ► painful awareness ("they realized they were naked")
- ► new self-sufficiency ("they sewed fig leaves together")
- ► the first experience of shame ("[they] made coverings for themselves").

naked: The Hebrew word carries the idea of being laid bare.[1] For example, one derivative of this word can be used to describe a bare, naked place—an unsheltered piece of land, exposed to the elements. The concept of complete openness and exposure is inherent in the word. In the context of Genesis 2:25 (God's giving of Eve to Adam), this becomes a highly relational word denoting utter candor between the two.

shame: Because Adam and Eve were completely open toward one another—nothing hidden—there was no cause for shame. Shame stems from having something to hide, something the revealing of which would be unbearable. Adam and Eve, before the Fall, were completely safe with one another because neither had any intention of using what he or she knew about the other in any harmful way.

coverings: The Hebrew word carries the idea of surrounding one's waist with a loin covering.[2] In other words, the covering's main purpose is to hide the sexual organs and thus to cover them as shameful. This does not imply that the sin of eating the fruit was a sexual sin. Rather, it implies that intimacy (symbolized by the sexual organs) would henceforth be connected with shame. No longer would it be possible to be completely open without the fear of becoming ashamed. The coverings, then, imply a lack of trust in one another and in God.

---

1. Francis Brown, S. R. Driver, and C. A. Briggs, *Hebrew and English Lexicon of the Old Testament* (Oxford: Clarendon Press, 1977), pp. 788-89.
2. Brown, Driver, and Briggs, pp. 291-92.

Session Four

Two Strange Roommates: Stress and Self-Condemnation

▼ ▼ ▼ ▼ ▼ ▼ ▼ ▼ ▼ ▼ ▼ ▼ ▼ ▼ ▼ ▼ ▼ ▼ ▼ ▼

Overview   10 minutes

❶ *Allow group members to share what they learned from the assignment. Then ask someone to read aloud this dialogue and the objectives that follow.*

Have you ever given someone a compliment only to have it fall flat? Here is a true-to-life dialogue between a father and his adolescent daughter:

> Father: You sure look nice today!
> Daughter: What?! My hair looks dead!
> Father: Well, I don't . . .
> Daughter: And my chin! Look how long it is. It makes my face way too long.
> Father: I don't see that. I think you're pretty.
> Daughter: Yeah, right. You're just trying to make me feel better.

This father walks away feeling that he never even had a chance to get through. He feels that the script his daughter was following was much more entrenched than any power he had to dislodge it. In this session we'll learn:

  ▶ the good news from Scripture about freedom in Christ from condemnation

41

➤ why we have such a hard time accepting that news
➤ how self-condemnation increases our stress

▼ ▼ ▼ ▼ ▼ ▼ ▼ ▼ ▼ ▼ ▼ ▼ ▼ ▼ ▼ ▼ ▼ ▼ ▼
Beginning   10 minutes

1. Why is it so hard for the daughter in the story above to accept her father's compliment? Or, put another way, why is it so hard, with regard to her appearance, to open up to hope?

2. The daughter is spoken of as having a "script" to follow. What scripts have you detected in your own life?
   I play the part of . . .

   ☐ an irresponsible little boy who doesn't want to have things required of him
   ☐ a clueless little girl who clings to others for protection
   ☐ a garbage receptacle for others' anger and criticism
   ☐ a doormat to whom others delegate their responsibilities
   ☐ a demanding bully who controls others or makes them pay
   ☐ an object (sexual or otherwise), someone who has no boundaries
   ☐ other:

3. How might these "scripts" be unnecessarily confining? How might each add to one's stress level?

▼ ▼ ▼ ▼ ▼ ▼ ▼ ▼ ▼ ▼ ▼ ▼ ▼ ▼ ▼ ▼ ▼ ▼
The Text   5 minutes
In the first seven chapters of Romans, Paul labors to establish that:
- ▶ every living soul is a sinner;
- ▶ no one can change that status by keeping God's laws;
- ▶ God's grace alone can change that status;
- ▶ grace is received through faith in Christ alone;
- ▶ grace should not lead to *more* sin but to an acting out of our loyalty to a new kingdom;
- ▶ this loyalty will be fiercely tested because we are at war within ourselves, a war between sin and righteousness.

The implied question at the end of Romans 7 is this: When sin wins inside me, will I be lost? Paul answers with a ringing cry:

There is therefore now **no condemnation** for those who are **in Christ Jesus**. For the law of the Spirit of life in Christ Jesus has set you free from the law of sin and death.

(Romans 8:1-2, NASB)

Later in the chapter, Paul reaffirms this:

Who will bring a **charge** against God's elect? God is the one who **justifies**; who is the one who condemns? Christ Jesus is He who died, yes, rather who was raised, who is at the right hand of God, who also intercedes for us.

(Romans 8:33-34, NASB)

A chosen one cannot be charged. Once God chooses us, we are safe forever from accusation.

▼ ▼ ▼ ▼ ▼ ▼ ▼ ▼ ▼ ▼ ▼ ▼ ▼ ▼ ▼ ▼ ▼ ▼
Understanding the Text   20 minutes

4. Paul says there is no condemnation. From whom?

5. Why is this so significant? If the Almighty God—the greatest
   One of all—does not condemn us, what does this say about
   lesser sources that might seek to condemn us?

6. Upon what basis have we been freed from condemnation?

7. In verse 33 Paul says no one can bring a charge against God's
   chosen ones. In what situations might we feel that charges are
   brought against us?

8. From what sources, other than God, might we fear condemnation?

9. According to verses 33-34, what does God do to offset the charges against us?

10. According to verses 33-34, what is Christ's role in God's plan to cancel the charges against us?

▼ ▼ ▼ ▼ ▼ ▼ ▼ ▼ ▼ ▼ ▼ ▼ ▼ ▼ ▼ ▼ ▼
Applying the Text   20 minutes

11. How would it change the "scripts" you follow if you really believed you were protected from *any* condemnation *whatsoever?*

12. What sources of condemnation do you struggle with most?
    ❑ voices inside me
    ❑ not living up to expectations (mine or others)
    ❑ family members
    ❑ my boss
    ❑ Satan
    ❑ I don't struggle with condemnation
    ❑ other:

Review the scripts under question 2. What is the role of condemnation (either of self or others) in these scripts? If we change the term "script" to "story," we could say that many people live out a life-story based on condemnation of self, others, or both.

13. a. If we're shooting ourselves full of condemnation, how might we be multiplying our stress?

    b. If we're shooting others full of condemnation, how might we be multiplying their stress?

❶ *Have one or two people read the following essay aloud.*

One reason we hate our limits (see chapter 2) is because they hamper us in our attempts to work off the charges against us. Another is that those limits themselves *become* further charges. Our shame kicks in, so we try to *hide* our limitations. Or, we try to *push beyond* our limits, spurred on by self-condemnation. Both *hiding* and *pushing beyond* increase our stress.

Let's say, though, that we succeed at both strategies and gain a certain amount of approval. Then what? *We don't rest in it.* Rather, we turn it into fuel for increased striving. How does this work? Approval provokes an anxious response: "If they really knew me [shame is talking here], they'd never approve of me. If they knew how hard I was having to work, they'd cancel their praise. So this approval is based only on my ability to both hide and push myself beyond limits." The approval, then, is reduced to a spur for even more anxious striving to (1) further hide our limitations and (2) push beyond them for more approval.

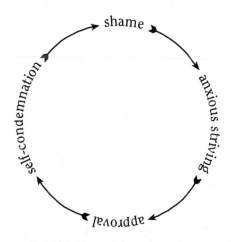

Where can we break this cycle? At the point of shame, because shame is fueled by accusation (see session 2 and its list of "not enoughs"). Our texts for this session come strongly to bear at this point by declaring that contemptuous, hateful accusation is never from God. Of course, God convicts and disciplines us when necessary, bringing light to our conscience. But His method is not that of Satan, the arch accuser.

47

Assignment   10 minutes

Take some time this week to meditate on Psalm 118:6:

> The LORD is for me; I will not fear;
> What can man do to me?

- ► What other words do you think of when you see the word "for" in this verse? Substitute as many of these words as you can in the verse. For example, "The Lord *supports* me."
- ► Because the Lord is for him, what does the psalmist resolve to do?
- ► How would you change the question in the second line into a statement?

Prayer   5 minutes

Allow everyone to complete the following statement:

The area in which I struggle most with self-condemnation is . . .

Let each person pray aloud, beginning with the leader. Pray for the person on your right by name, based on the statements that have been made. If you would rather pray silently, please say "Amen" aloud to let the other people know you are finished.

▼ ▼

Reference Notes

no condemnation: A key to interpreting this phrase lies in Romans 7:4: "Therefore, my brethren, you also were made to die to the Law through the body of Christ, that you might be joined to another, to Him who was raised from the dead, that we might bear fruit for God."[1] Because we have died to the Law, it no longer has jurisdiction over us as a condemning agent.[2] Moreover, we have been joined to Christ, who has taken on all condemnation due us under the Law. There is simply no longer any basis upon which God would reject us, despite our continued failure to live up to His standards.

in Christ Jesus: This phrase is basically shorthand for our being identified with Christ in His death and resurrection (see Romans 6:1-11).

charge: This word indicates that Paul envisioned a courtroom scene, a place of judgment. Possibly he has Satan's role as accuser in mind.[3] The idea is that no one, not even Satan, can bring a valid accusation against God's chosen ones.

justifies: The Greek word here means "to declare or pronounce righteous," the idea being that God, on the basis of Christ's atonement, declares fully righteous those who trust in Christ and His work on their behalf. This is God's act of pure grace.

---

1. C. E. B. Cranfield, *The Epistle to the Romans*, Vol. I, International Critical Commentaries (Edinburgh: T & T Clark, 1975), p. 372.
2. Cranfield, p. 373.
3. Cranfield, p. 438.

Session Five

Learning to Live Away from Home

▼ ▼ ▼ ▼ ▼ ▼ ▼ ▼ ▼ ▼ ▼ ▼ ▼ ▼ ▼ ▼ ▼ ▼

Overview   10 minutes

❶ *Allow group members to share what they learned from their homework. Then ask someone to read the following story and objectives aloud.*

Recently, a man told me a story about working for his father. (He was eighteen when this took place.)

"One day," he said, "I was working really hard. It was a sweaty, nasty job; and I took a couple of breaks to cool off. But I went at it hard all day. That afternoon, my dad came to my workstation and invited me to join him for a burger after work. I was elated. This rarely happened, just the two of us. I hoped he was feeling good about my work effort. When we got to the burger place, he sat me down and said, 'I've noticed your work is pretty sloppy. I don't want you setting a bad example for others by taking too many breaks.' I was stunned. So far from my hopes being realized, I was being rebuked as a slacker. Surprising even myself, I burst into tears. My father's response? A snort of disgust as he turned away."

As I listened, I heard an aching man still trying to digest a pain he'd felt for twenty years. Why must life hurt so? In this session, we'll learn:

> ▶ how we're designed for another world, though we don't yet have the opportunity to live there

51

- ▶ how that discrepancy induces an unavoidable ache
- ▶ how we mismanage that ache and end up overstressed
- ▶ how God wants to use that ache

Beginning   10 minutes

1. What would an eighteen-year-old boy so deeply want from his father that he'd burst into tears when he couldn't get it?

2. How might a father become so out of tune with what his son legitimately wants?

3. How do you suppose the eighteen-year-old was feeling that evening after he'd met with his father?

      Generation after generation, people live and die with powerful unmet yearnings. What does this say about what might be going on inside of people?

The Text   5 minutes

❶ *Have someone in the group read the following text. The group also may read the reference notes on pages 58-59.*

In session 3 we saw how Adam and Eve learned to feel shame and fear in each other's presence after they disobeyed God. They tried to hide from each other. The story goes on to recount how they hid from God as well. God found them and declared other consequences of their act: all the central experiences of human life would be flavored with suffering. But God took action to ensure that this life of futility would not go on forever.

To the woman he [God] said:
"I will greatly increase your pains in childbearing;
    with pain you will give birth to children.
Your desire will be for your husband,
    and he will rule over you."
To Adam he said, "Because you listened to your wife and ate from the tree about which I commanded you, 'You must not eat of it,'
"Cursed is the ground because of you;
    through painful toil you will eat of it
    all the days of your life.
It will produce thorns and thistles for you,
    and you will eat of the plants of the field.
By the sweat of your brow
    you will eat your food
until you return to the ground,
    since from it you were taken;
for dust you are
    and to dust you will return." . . .

And the LORD God said, "The man has now become like **one of us**, knowing good and evil. He must not be allowed to reach out his hand and take also from **the tree of life** and eat, and **live forever.**" So the LORD God **banished him** from the Garden of Eden, to **work the ground** from which he had been taken. After he drove the man out, he placed on the east side of the Garden of

Eden cherubim and a flaming sword flashing back and forth to guard the way to the tree of life.

(Genesis 3:16-19, 22-24)

God was graciously concerned lest the man (and woman) "stretch out his hand . . . and eat, and live forever." To protect them from living forever in their sinful condition, God expelled them from the garden. They were safe from irreversible consequences. On the other hand, the leave-taking had to be painful for the man and woman. All the blessings of closeness with God were lost. The perfect nest at the very apex of creation had to be forsaken. The delightful world for which God intended them was closed forever. Exiled into a fallen world for which they were poorly suited, they entered an ache and a homesickness that we also have inherited.

▼ ▼ ▼ ▼ ▼ ▼ ▼ ▼ ▼ ▼ ▼ ▼ ▼ ▼ ▼ ▼ ▼ ▼ ▼

Understanding the Text   15 minutes

4. What effects did Adam and Eve's rebellion have on each of these aspects of life?

    ❏ marriage
    ❏ childbearing
    ❏ work

5. Imagine yourself in Adam and Eve's place. You know you were made for relationships without shame, but now there is shame between you. Eve desires Adam's love, but Adam dominates her. You were made to be fruitful and multiply, but now childbearing is excruciatingly painful. You were made to tend a beautiful garden, but now every day you have to labor in a field of thorns and thistles. What would you feel in this situation? What would you do?

6. What sources of stress do you see in this passage?

7. God prevented Adam and Eve from living forever in these circumstances. Do you think this was a blessing or a punishment? Why?

▼ ▼ ▼ ▼ ▼ ▼ ▼ ▼ ▼ ▼ ▼ ▼ ▼ ▼ ▼ ▼ ▼ ▼ ▼

Applying the Text   20 minutes

8. Genesis 3 implies that we're all homesick for Eden. Can anything this world provides fully remove that ache? Why or why not?

9. Christians have met the way home: Jesus Christ. But we're not home yet. In fact, we still live in a cursed world that increases our ache. Are you aware of an ache inside you? For example, what ache do you become aware of when you think of:

❏ your relationships with your spouse, children, friends, or parents
❏ broken dreams and disappointments
❏ your work

10. How do you seek to manage this ache?

❏ I work harder and harder to get my husband to notice me. It hurts too much to stop and admit the truth.
❏ I try to make enough money to silence that voice in my head that says, "You'll never amount to anything."
❏ I work to be a nice guy, to leave a good taste in everyone's mouth so they won't reject me.

❒ I crave applause and attention and will do about anything to get it. Being ignored would throw me into overwhelming loneliness.

❒ I'm not aware of any ache.

❒ Other:

11. Think about the above examples of managing our ache. How might trying to manage our ache actually increase our stress?

12. Instead of managing our ache, how else might we respond to it?

13. Many of us avoid taking our ache to God. If we hide it from God, what might that say about how we see Him? Here are some possibilities:

❒ God says He loves me, but you can't trust what people say.

❒ God is like everyone else: behind the appearance of forgiveness, He is angry and disappointed with me.

❒ God is far away. My prayers never reach Him.

❒ God is critical and demanding. I cannot possibly meet His standards.

❒ God has grown tired with me. I've prayed about the same stuff so often that He's probably tuned me out.

❒ Because God knows my deepest sins, I can't bear to see His scowl.

❐ God isn't concerned about how I feel; He's concerned with His agenda: building His kingdom.

❐ Other:

❶ *Have someone read the following essay aloud.*

Exploring the ache inside can lead to a constructive exhaustion ("I am tired of trying to beat this world into the shape I want it to take") that, when paired with faith ("I want to trust and know God as He truly is, rather than trying to hammer the world into something it can't be"), emerges as perseverance (going deeper into knowing God and waiting patiently for the development of godly character—see James 1:2-4).

On the other hand, ignoring the ache leads to anxious performing that generates a destructive exhaustion known as burnout. Exploring the ache, not ignoring it, helps us to see that the ache is simply too deep to be touched by momentary, manipulated affirmations from others.

▼ ▼ ▼ ▼ ▼ ▼ ▼ ▼ ▼ ▼ ▼ ▼ ▼ ▼ ▼ ▼ ▼ ▼
Assignment   5 minutes

Elective 1: Reflection—Think back to the eighteen-year-old from the beginning of our session. Assume he is living with a high degree of stress, so much so that it prompted him to see a counselor. Using Genesis 3:22-24, develop three things you'd want to say to this man (now in his late thirties) to help him think through the relationship between his stress and his feelings about his father.

Elective 2: Reflection—Read Genesis 3:14-19 and reflect on the following questions:

▶ Why do you think God cursed childbirth and the husband-wife relationship for the woman, while, for the man, he cursed the ground from which the man was to get his food?

▶ In what deep ways have both a woman's and a man's worlds been made harder by these curses? What might this say about the respective stresses a woman or man might feel?

▼ ▼ ▼ ▼ ▼ ▼ ▼ ▼ ▼ ▼ ▼ ▼ ▼ ▼ ▼ ▼ ▼ ▼ ▼

Reference Notes

one of us: Here God may be speaking to the angels, the heavenly court, as he does in Job 1:6–2:6. Or He could be speaking of Himself in the plural. Kings often speak of themselves in this way, and God is also Triune: Father, Son, and Holy Spirit.

the tree of life: There were two trees in the middle of the garden (Genesis 2:9). The tree of the knowledge of good and evil was the forbidden one from which the first couple ate.

live forever: God was not concerned with man living forever *per se*, but with his living forever in a permanent state of sin. Had this happened, man and woman would have been alienated from God forever. In His mercy, God drove man and woman out of the garden. His goal was to put them in a position to be redeemed.

banished him: This word is forceful in the Hebrew. God is decisive here; He knows what is at stake. To redeem man and woman, He had to keep them redeemable.

work the ground: Adam is sent out to cultivate the very ground from which he came (see Genesis 2:7). In this, he is reminded of his mortality and his dependency on God. He also is placed in direct contact with the curse and is reminded constantly of his limits, his temptation to go beyond those limits, and his desperate need to know God.

▼ ▼

Additional Resource

Crabb, Larry. *The Silence of Adam*. Grand Rapids, Mich.:
   Zondervan, 1995.

Session Six
Self-Inflicted Stress and Its Offspring, Burnout

▼ ▼
Overview   10 minutes

O *Allow group members to share what they learned from their homework. Then ask someone to read aloud this story and the objectives that follow.*

Pastor Clark was getting sick of these nagging dizzy spells. Last Sunday, he'd found himself holding onto the pulpit with one hand during the last five minutes of his sermon. The week before that, in a counseling session, he'd spaced out for a few minutes and missed a key point the distraught man was making. Just a touch of dizziness, he'd thought. No big deal. But now his left arm was numb half the time, and the dizzy spells were coming more often. He didn't have time for this. He'd just have to get up a little earlier and pray another fifteen minutes over this weird dizziness. And he'd *really* have to brace himself during the upcoming baptismal service. Fifteen people were planning to be immersed.

With a deep sigh he fought to bring his attention back to the outline he was preparing. Why was it growing so difficult to concentrate? He'd never had this much trouble powering through stressful periods before. . . .

In this session we'll learn:

- ► the alarm/endurance/exhaustion sequence of stress
- ► how overcoming the evil of a fallen world with the evil of self-sufficiency violates Romans 12:21

61

▶ how it looks to move from intense performance to loving well.

▼ ▼
Beginning   15 minutes

Pastor Clark has reached the last stage of a three-part sequence. Look at this diagram:

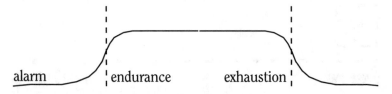

alarm ⎸ endurance   exhaustion ⎸

   The curve shows three stages of responding to stress. First, one's system is aroused to make massive adjustments to the stressor. This is what happens, for example, when the heart speeds up to adjust to the body's demand for oxygen during exercise.

   Second, the system adjusts to the continuing demands made by the stressor and keeps readjusting to those demands. As one keeps exercising, the heart sustains its speedy pace by pulling on reserves of strength within its own muscular structure.

   Third, the system uses up all available reserves and can no longer adjust to the stressor. This stage of exhaustion quickly leads to the breakdown of the system. The heart, for example, may go into arrhythmia or into arrest in response to prolonged overload.

   Pastor Clark shows signs of moving into the exhaustion stage.

1. Where would you put yourself on the diagram we just looked at? What are your reasons for placing yourself where you did?

2. What signs of exhaustion do you see in your life, if any? (Such signs might include chronic heartburn, tension headaches, pain in the shoulder blades, joylessness, chronic fatigue/low energy, a feeling of being chased by your schedule, endless time urgency, and anger at interruptions or basic requests like, "Dad/Mom, can I play with you?")

▼ ▼ ▼ ▼ ▼ ▼ ▼ ▼ ▼ ▼ ▼ ▼ ▼ ▼ ▼ ▼ ▼ ▼ ▼

The Text   5 minutes

❶ *Have someone read the following material aloud. You may also want to give people a chance to look over the reference notes on pages 69-70.*

The gospel always represents a disorienting freedom. It causes a deeply ingrained part of us such initial discomfort that we long to go back to some self-sufficient way of life. (For example, the Galatian believers were free from slavish adherence to the Law, but they quickly abandoned their freedom in favor of comfortable legal bondage.) The writer of Hebrews is addressing disrupted people. They want to go back to the steadying worship of angels, back to the structures of Moses. The message of Hebrews (particularly the passage below) is, "Don't go back. Don't re-enter the arrogance of working things out *your* way. Rest in God. Trust Him when you're most afraid. Let Him be the reason for stopping your anxious striving."

There remains, then, a **Sabbath-rest** for the people of God; for anyone who enters God's rest also **rests from his own work,** just as God did from his. Let us, therefore, **make every effort to enter that rest**, so that no one will fall by following their [Israel's] example of **disobedience**.

(Hebrews 4:9-11)

To rest is to count on God to be the protective reality rather than engineering our own.

Understanding the Text   15 minutes

3. a. What does the writer mean when he speaks of a "Sabbath-rest" for God's people?

   b. In what sense is this rest something we look forward to in the future?

   c. In what sense is this rest available to us now?

4. The writer says that "disobedience" can block a person from entering God's rest. What sort of disobedience do you think he has in mind?

Hebrews 3:19 adds, "So we see that they [the Israelites] were not able to enter [God's rest], because of their unbelief." Unbelief is as big a problem as disobedience—in fact, the two are linked.

5. What does one have to believe about God to rest completely in Him?

▼ ▼ ▼ ▼ ▼ ▼ ▼ ▼ ▼ ▼ ▼ ▼ ▼ ▼ ▼ ▼ ▼
Applying the Text   20 minutes
6. How might stress reflect difficulties in truly believing God?

7. Many of the nouns and pronouns in the text are plural ("people," "us," "their"). The writer envisions a community effort aimed at entering God's rest. How does close fellowship with each other help us to enter God's rest?

8. In Hebrews 3:13 he writes, "But encourage one another daily . . . so that none of you may be hardened by sin's deceitfulness." How—in practical terms—can we help one another enter the rest God has for us?

One of Jesus' names is "Immanuel," which means "God with us." God has come near in Christ. Because He has come close to us, we are to come close to *each other*. Why? So that none of us struggles alone in his or her efforts to respond to God's call. We will never struggle successfully if we struggle alone. God has called us home, and we're fellow pilgrims, encouraging one another along the way.

9. How acceptable is it to you to struggle as a Christian? Explain your reasoning to the group.

10. How might letting our struggles be known to one another help decrease the stresses in our lives?

11. Each of us has our own brand of self-sufficiency. What does self-sufficiency look like in your life?

12. We've said that "the gospel causes a deeply ingrained part of us such discomfort that we long to go back to some self-sufficient way of life." What do you think prompts our deep commitment to self-sufficiency, to being the captain of our own ships? What might living in a fallen world have to do with this commitment?

❶ *Have someone read the following essay aloud.*

Why is rest so hard to embrace, so threatening? Partly because of the value we put on hard work and partly because of the anxiety of protecting and providing for ourselves and our families. To be invited into rest is to be invited to lay down one's arms (self-sufficiency) in the very midst of a conflict (facing the harshness of a fallen world). Can God be trusted?

To rest is to count on God to protect us rather than making it happen ourselves. Something must help us bear the pain of living in a fallen world. Most of us opt for our own abilities to assuage that pain. We develop a style of self-sufficiency, and it is the opposite of resting. The more we cling to self-sufficiency, the more stress we'll experience.

Assignment   5 minutes

Elective 1: Reflection— At the top of a clean sheet of paper, write the title, "How I Try to Make This World Work on My Own Terms." Then start brainstorming. Set a timer for fifteen minutes, and during that time, just write. Write whatever comes to mind, nonstop, without worrying about spelling or grammar. Think about self-sufficient survival efforts you attempt in your family relationships, in your work, in your social life. Then take the results to the Lord in prayer, asking Him to show you areas that call for repentance.

Elective 2: Project—

► Keep a notebook on yourself for a week. At the end of each day, jot down those ways in which, looking back, you can see yourself trying to be self-sufficient instead of trusting God.

► Ask your spouse to keep a notebook on you for the same purpose.

► Watch a television show or movie and keep track of choices and actions in the characters that reflect self-sufficiency.

Prayer   5 minutes

Self-sufficiency always gets in the way of knowing God (and knowing Him is the key to being still, according to Psalm 46:10). Allow each person in the group to choose one of the following statements:

► When I think of my own self-sufficiency, I draw a blank. I simply don't know what it looks like.

► My style of self-sufficiency is beginning to dawn on me.

► My style of self-sufficiency is pretty clear to me, but I don't know for sure what repentance looks like.

> ► I know what my style of self-sufficiency looks like and
> what repentance would entail, but I'm terrified.
> ► I would like to be less self-sufficient in the area of . . .

Let each person pray aloud, beginning with the leader. Pray
for the person on your right, based on the statements that have
been made. If you would rather pray silently, please say "Amen"
aloud to let the other people know you are finished.

▼ ▼ ▼ ▼ ▼ ▼ ▼ ▼ ▼ ▼ ▼ ▼ ▼ ▼ ▼ ▼ ▼ ▼ ▼

Reference Notes

Setting: The book of Hebrews was written for Jewish followers of
Christ who were under pressure from other Jews to renounce their
faith in Christ. The question facing these believers was whether
they would seek security with God through the ancient Jewish rit-
uals or by putting their entire trust in Christ.

Most of us today are much more tempted to seek security
through frenetic activity: long hours at work, sports, arts and
computer classes for our kids, serving at church. Just as Jewish
ritual in itself is not ungodly, so hard work in itself is not ungodly.
But to rely on either ritual or activity for our security, rather than
on Christ, blocks us from entering the rest that God promises
humankind from the book of Genesis onward.

The writer of Hebrews illustrates his point with the Old Testament story of the Israelites in the desert with Moses. This story
would have been familiar to the Hebrews. Back then, the Israelites
were trying to enter the "rest" of the Promised Land, but God prevented a whole generation from entering it because of their disobedience and lack of trust. In the same way, says the writer, our
disobedience and unbelief can block us from entering God's rest (the
Promised Land, a restful state now, or the future rest of eternal life).

Sabbath-rest: The Greek word literally means "a Sabbath-
keeping." God commanded the Israelites to work for six days and
then avoid work on the seventh day as a sign that they trusted
God, rather than their hard work, to provide for them. The Sab-
bath became a symbol of the complete rest God would someday

bring when His kingdom was fulfilled. Although that complete rest has not yet been fulfilled, we can enter now into a foretaste of it. A restful state of mind, heart, and action is available to us to the degree that we put our trust fully in Christ. So when we read the word "rest," we should think both of the future rest and the presently available rest.

rests from his own work: Just as God ceased His work of creation on the seventh day, so we can rest from self-effort, from going back to the tried-and-true self-sufficiency on which we've relied in the past. (We also have the privilege of resting from the activity and work we do that is not driven by self-sufficiency!)

make every effort to enter that rest: We are to be earnest, diligent, and eager to enter God's rest, to quit trusting in our own works, our own self-sufficiency.

disobedience: To refuse to listen or be persuaded. It includes the hardening of one's heart so that truth cannot enter.

▼ ▼ ▼ ▼ ▼ ▼ ▼ ▼ ▼ ▼ ▼ ▼ ▼ ▼ ▼ ▼ ▼ ▼
Additional Resources

Allender, Dan B., and Tremper Longman, III. *Cry of the Soul.* Colorado Springs, Colo.: NavPress, 1994.
Crabb, Larry. *Finding God.* Grand Rapids, Mich.: Zondervan, 1993.

▼ ▼ ▼ ▼ ▼ ▼ ▼ ▼ ▼ ▼ ▼ ▼ ▼ ▼ ▼ ▼ ▼ ▼
Food for Thought

"I am now beckoned to replace *doubt* and its companions, terror and rage, with a *confidence* in God's character that frees me to relax and trust (see Isaiah 30:15). I can then do a little better job of moving toward others without demanding what God has already given. . . . Instead of saying "I need you," I say, "I want to give something good to you. I want you to relax in the strength that is slowly freeing me to remain confident and hopeful no matter how bad I feel or what struggles come my way."

—Larry Crabb,
Finding God,
p. 116

Session Seven
Hope of Resolution

▼ ▼ ▼ ▼ ▼ ▼ ▼ ▼ ▼ ▼ ▼ ▼ ▼ ▼ ▼ ▼ ▼ ▼ ▼
Overview   10 minutes

❶ *Allow group members to share what they learned from their homework or recap what they learned from last session. Then ask someone to read aloud this story and the objectives that follow.*

There was a great split among the otters. The oil spill caused it. Some wanted to leave their home territory and head for the open sea, get out of the oil spill entirely. Others thought living at home all-important and declared they'd never leave, that they'd, by golly, learn to adjust to the slimy environs.

Some adapted to life in the slime while others headed for the open sea. Years later, the open-sea cousins came back to check on their adaptive relatives. The oil-slick crowd was proud that they'd learned to live with dyspepsia from eating befouled shellfish. But the open-sea cousins were sad and appalled.

"Why," they asked, "would you want to live like this? Head for the open sea!"

But their cousins replied, "The open sea is a dangerous place. Besides, we've had to be pretty sharp to make life work here. And it's not half-bad."

The open-sea relatives were aghast: "You'd rather look clever than be free from all this?"

The adapters were not put off, "Not so fast. Free is risky. Besides, clever has its rewards. How many can say they've survived the oil as we have?"

We find ourselves cheering for the open-sea bunch. Like them, we long to be free from our foul, sad imprisonment in this world. But then we realize something: We *can't* "head for the open sea." That would amount to escaping this world altogether and heading for heaven! Right now, we're stuck here. But is it possible to gain new freedom *within* this difficult world? In this session we'll learn:

▶ How to adjust our appetites and desires to those of God's kingdom.

▶ How we all live in the pain of imprisonment yet have the freedom not to overcome evil with evil.

▶ How accepting some limits (and bursting free from others) can free us to enjoy God and convey His love to others. We go from trying to impress others to seeking to serve them.

▼ ▼ ▼ ▼ ▼ ▼ ▼ ▼ ▼ ▼ ▼ ▼ ▼ ▼ ▼ ▼ ▼ ▼
Beginning   20 minutes

1. Why were the otters who stayed in the oil slick afraid of freedom? What were the risks of becoming more free?

2. How might seeking freedom be risky in your life?

☐ If I tell my spouse how I really feel (freedom), she might leave me (risk).

☐ If I tell my spouse about this problem I've never shared (freedom), his walls might go higher than ever (risk).

☐ If I go back to school to finish my degree (freedom), I might fail—it's been so long since I've studied (risk).

☐ If I learn to dance (freedom), I might never get it quite right and look really stupid (risk).

☐ Other:

3. How have you found safety in the oil slick of life?

4. Has your strategy for safety hindered your joy or increased your stress in any ways? If so, how?

We need to accept some of our limits (session 2), but we need to escape others. Generally, we need to:

▶ 1. accept those things in ourselves of which others have been ashamed

▶ 2. determine how we, as a result, perceive ourselves in distorted ways

▶ 3. escape the limits imposed over the years by (1) and (2) above.

5. What limits do you need to escape? Take five minutes to write down your thoughts. Then share them with the group. The leader should go first.

a. Things about which others have been ashamed in me:

b. Distorted ideas I've had of myself, because of the above:

c. Limits I need to escape:

▼ ▼ ▼ ▼ ▼ ▼ ▼ ▼ ▼ ▼ ▼ ▼ ▼ ▼ ▼ ▼ ▼ ▼ ▼
The Text   5 minutes

The Pharisees are angry with Jesus (as usual). Why are they so
miffed? It's because "This man welcomes sinners and eats with
them" (Luke 15:2). In response, Jesus tells three stories about finding lost things. First, there is a lost sheep found by the compas-
sionate shepherd. Then there is a lost coin found by the diligent
woman. Finally, a lost son is found by a gracious, delighted father.
But before this son can be found, he loses himself thoroughly.

Jesus continued, "There was a man who had two sons. The
younger one said to his father, '**Father, give me my share of the
estate.**' So he divided his property between them.
Not long after that, the younger son got together all he had,
set off for a distant country and there squandered his wealth in
wild living. After he had spent everything, there was a severe
famine in that whole country, and he began to be in need. So he
went and hired himself out to a citizen of that country, who sent
him to his fields to **feed pigs**. He longed to fill his stomach with
the pods that the pigs were eating, but no one gave him anything.
(Luke 15:11-16)

Understanding the Text   15 minutes

6. A few sentences into the story, Jesus says the son "began to be in need." But how did this son show his neediness right at the beginning of the story?

7. What was his foolish solution to that neediness?

8. Very soon it became clear that this son's solution would not work. He spent all he had. How do you think the Jewish audience would have heard the phrase "to feed pigs"?

9. What does this story suggest about the results of trying to meet our needs in our own foolish ways?

10. What were the sources of stress on this son as he worked to feed the pigs?

11. "He longed to fill his stomach." This is, in part, a story about appetite. How had this son's appetites ruled him at first? And how did they end up ruling him?

12. What do you think Jesus wants us to learn about appetites and needs?

▼ ▼ ▼ ▼ ▼ ▼ ▼ ▼ ▼ ▼ ▼ ▼ ▼ ▼ ▼ ▼ ▼ ▼
Applying the Text   20 minutes

13. What are some things on which you have set your desires in this life?

14. When you think of the objects of your desires, how big are they in comparison with God?

15. Why do you suppose most of us would rather keep our appetites and desires relatively small? How does this help make life more manageable?

16. Instead of managing life, we could depend more deeply on Life Himself. What might that look like for you?

17. What risks would that involve?

18. a. What freedoms might you then have?

b. What limits might you accept?

c. How might this lower your stress?

❶ *Have one or two people read the following essay aloud.*

C. S. Lewis writes, "No doubt all our desires make promises [to us]. . . ."[1] He means our desires tell us that if we go ahead and satisfy them, they will deliver a great and lasting happiness to us. It's this promise at the heart of every desire that distracts us. The siren song of these promises draws us away from God, who promises blessing to His children. But His promises are those of Another who is outside our control. We are tempted by the promises within our own desires, those promises we can control and manage.

We keep forgetting that the promises we make to ourselves all too often prove untrue. We listen to those promises, says Lewis, "not because of what our passion shows itself to be in experience but because of what it professes to be while we are in its grip."[2] The prodigal son felt both the desire and the promise embodied within the money he demanded from his father. In the grip of desire he believed the wild illusion of free living without consequences, content within himself. In the sober light of experience, he knew the promise was a lie. That it was a lie was proved in the nearby pigs rooting in the soil. When our appetites are too small, when they are formed by our own desires and promises apart from God, we are duped. Living under the lie that those promises will be fulfilled, we are deeply stressed. It is always stressful to live in an illusion.

▼ ▼ ▼ ▼ ▼ ▼ ▼ ▼ ▼ ▼ ▼ ▼ ▼ ▼ ▼ ▼ ▼ ▼

Assignment   5 minutes

Elective 1: Reflection—Jot down some thoughts in a journal about how you have kept your desires relatively small and how that has made you both more self-sufficient and more stressed.

Elective 2: Project—Head a sheet of paper, "How My Desires Might Point Me to God." G. K. Chesterton said, "The man who knocks on the door of a brothel is looking for God." How do desires, no matter how wrong or right, indicate that we are made for God? Write down five desires that have marked your life. Then explore each of them, writing down how they might point to a deep thirst for God. For help here, read Isaiah 55:1-3.

▼ ▼ ▼ ▼ ▼ ▼ ▼ ▼ ▼ ▼ ▼ ▼ ▼ ▼ ▼ ▼ ▼ ▼

Prayer   5 minutes

Allow each person to ask briefly for one prayer request concerning this session. Let each person pray aloud for the person on his or her right, beginning with the leader. Pray for each other by name. If you would rather pray silently, please say "Amen" aloud to let the other people know you are finished.

▼ ▼ ▼ ▼ ▼ ▼ ▼ ▼ ▼ ▼ ▼ ▼ ▼ ▼ ▼ ▼ ▼ ▼

Reference Notes

Father, give me my share of the estate: In asking not only for his share of the estate, but also for the right to spend it, the son is, in effect, saying, "Father, I cannot wait for you to die."[3] The request is even more offensive than it looks on the surface.

feed pigs: According to the Law of Moses, pigs were unclean animals and could not be eaten. A Jewish audience would have been aghast at the degradation to which this man had sunk.

▼ ▼ ▼ ▼ ▼ ▼ ▼ ▼ ▼ ▼ ▼ ▼ ▼ ▼ ▼ ▼ ▼ ▼
Additional Resources

Houston, James. *The Heart's Desire: Satisfying the Hunger of the Soul*. Colorado Springs, Colo.: NavPress, 1996.
Nouwen, Henri J. M. *The Return of the Prodigal Son*. New York: Doubleday, 1992.

▼ ▼ ▼ ▼ ▼ ▼ ▼ ▼ ▼ ▼ ▼ ▼ ▼ ▼ ▼ ▼ ▼ ▼
Food for Thought

"As long as God appears to work through channels we can control, our comfortable status is still quo."

—David Swartz,
Dancing with Broken Bones
(Colorado Springs, Colo.: NavPress, 1987),
p. 148

---

1. C. S. Lewis, *God in the Dock* (Grand Rapids, Mich.: Eerdmans, 1970), p. 320.
2. Lewis, p. 321.
3. Kenneth E. Bailey, *Poet and Peasant and Through Peasant Eyes: A Literary-Cultural Approach to the Parables* (Grand Rapids, Mich.: Eerdmans, 1983), pp. 161-62, cited in Henri J. M. Nouwen, *The Return of the Prodigal Son* (New York: Doubleday, 1992), p. 36.

Session Eight
Turning for Home

▼ ▼ ▼ ▼ ▼ ▼ ▼ ▼ ▼ ▼ ▼ ▼ ▼ ▼ ▼ ▼ ▼ ▼
Overview   10 minutes

❶ *Allow group members to share what they learned from their homework or recap what they learned from the last session. Then ask someone to read aloud this story and the objectives that follow.*

I led a men's retreat recently. For many reasons, I was particularly anxious about how this one would go. The first session was on a Friday night. Although I poured myself into it, the group seemed a bit subdued—that is to say, dead. I tried to rescue the session by saying a really dynamic prayer at the end, but that, too, fell flat. I left the session feeling spent and dreading the Saturday morning session to come.

That night, I wrestled with myself and with God. I was filled with anxiety about the coming day. My desire for validation hadn't been met in the previous session. What if things just got worse? What if I kept falling flat? What if the men sat out there thinking, "I can't believe they hired this guy. What a waste of a weekend"? My fears were running away with me, but what was their source? Subtly, I had allowed my desire for validation to eclipse my longing to follow God and offer Him to these men. At the heart of my desire was a promise. It went something like this: "If you can perform well, these men will affirm you, and that will provide immediate happiness you can feed on for a long time." But there's a downside to the promise as well, "If you perform badly, you'll be held in contempt, and the shame you'll feel will poison your soul for a long time."

Principle: If I'm going to be in charge of my own blessing, then I'll have to take the curses that come if I fail.

Of course, God wants me under no such arrangement. He wants to be in charge, wants to bless, wants me to relinquish my desires to Him (Isaiah 55:1-3). In this session we'll learn:

▶ To turn away from egocentric anxiety through both spirituality and community

▶ About the "banquet" God has for those who trust Him with their deepest desires

▶ About the "curses" under which we labor when we insist on managing our own desires

▶ How these "curses" increase our stress

▼ ▼ ▼ ▼ ▼ ▼ ▼ ▼ ▼ ▼ ▼ ▼ ▼ ▼ ▼ ▼ ▼ ▼ ▼

Beginning   10 minutes

1. What are some things about which you feel anxious?

❑ finances
❑ aging
❑ job/career questions
❑ a key relationship declining
❑ what's waiting for you at work tomorrow
❑ feeling trapped in a situation (job, relationship, educational limitations)
❑ performance (parenting, on the job, sexually, in your spiritual life, in social settings)
❑ other:

Anxiety is often egocentric. That is, it reflects that I'm living in the tension between the fulfillment of self-generated promise and curse. I don't know the outcome yet, but I know if I fail, the curse will hit hard. I've got to prevent that, but I don't know if I can. That's anxiety!

2. When have you lived in that tension recently? How did the tension affect your stress level?

3. What might you learn from these anxieties about what you desire?

▼ ▼ ▼ ▼ ▼ ▼ ▼ ▼ ▼ ▼ ▼ ▼ ▼ ▼ ▼ ▼ ▼ ▼

The Text   5 minutes

The prodigal son has been feeding the pigs for awhile now. He is tired and hungry. No one will help him. Fortunately, that's not the end of the story. Let's talk about his story again.

There was a man who had two sons. The younger one said to his father, "Father, give me my share of the estate." So he divided his property between them.

Not long after that, the younger son got together all he had, set off for a distant country, and there squandered his wealth in wild living. After he had spent everything, there was a severe famine in that whole country, and he began to be in need. So he went and hired himself out to a citizen of that country, who sent him to his fields to feed pigs. He longed to fill his stomach with the pods that the pigs were eating, but no one gave him anything.

When he came to his senses, he said, "How many of my father's hired men have food to spare, and here I am starving to death! I will set out and go back to my father and say to him:

Father, I have sinned against heaven and against you. I am no longer worthy to be called your son; make me like one of your hired men." So he got up and went to his father.

But while he was still a long way off, his father saw him and was filled with compassion for him; **he ran** to his son, threw his arms around him and kissed him.

The son said to him, "Father, I have sinned against heaven and against you. I am no longer worthy to be called your son."

But the father said to his servants, "Quick! Bring the best **robe** and put it on him. Put a **ring** on his finger and **sandals** on his feet. Bring the fattened calf and kill it. Let's have a feast and celebrate. For this son of mine was dead and is alive again; **he was lost and is found**." So they began to celebrate.

(Luke 15:11-24)

Come, all you who are thirsty,
   come to the waters;
and you who have no money,
   come, buy and eat!
Come, buy wine and milk
   without money and without cost.
Why spend your money for what is not bread,
   and your labor for what does not satisfy?
Listen, listen to me, and eat what is good,
   and your soul will delight in the richest of fare.
Give ear and come to me;
   hear me, that your soul may live.

(Isaiah 55:1-3)

▼ ▼ ▼ ▼ ▼ ▼ ▼ ▼ ▼ ▼ ▼ ▼ ▼ ▼ ▼ ▼ ▼ ▼
Understanding the Text   15 minutes

When disappointed desire comes home repentantly, it is not punished but is graciously met with abundance, an abundance that was always there but was unnoticed because of unbelief.

One of our goals in this session is to learn how spirituality and community can help us to turn from egocentric anxiety. Let's think about the spirituality part for a minute. There are many ways to practice Christian spirituality. The following ways are aimed especially at reducing self-sufficiency by diminishing unnecessary stress. Use the chart below to think through this mode of spirituality.

<u>Accept Limits</u>
I can never become "enough" to make life work the way I think it should. This is the way of *honesty*.

<u>Accept Costs</u>
I'll have to go without some of the things this world offers. This is the way of *repentance*.

<u>Transcend Limits</u>
Only heaven will be enough. I'll tune my appetites to heaven. This is the way of *discipleship*.

<u>Transcend Costs</u>
The supplies of heaven are utterly free (see Isaiah 55:1-3). God has given me a down payment on these riches through the Holy Spirit. This is the way of *hope*.

4. How was the prodigal son honest with himself?

5. How does he show that he decided to live without some of the things the world offers?

6. What do you think it was like for him to sit down to a banquet after longing for pig food day after day?

7. How did the prodigal son live out Isaiah 55:1-3?

8. The prodigal prepared a speech for his father. Which part of the speech did the father listen to? Which part did he preclude? What, do you think, is the significance of this?

▼ ▼ ▼ ▼ ▼ ▼ ▼ ▼ ▼ ▼ ▼ ▼ ▼ ▼ ▼ ▼ ▼
Applying the Text   20 minutes

9. The prodigal son "came to his senses." He realized that, after all his planning and striving, he was much worse off than when he began. Are there places in your life where planning and striving in your own strength have left you worse off? What desires drove that planning and striving?

10. Refer to the chart on page 87 as you reflect on these questions.

   a. How might God be calling on you to be honest about your commitment to self-sufficiency?

b. What are some things—both tangible and intangible—God might be calling you to do without?

c. How might forsaking the pursuit of those things reduce your stress level?

d. In what ways have your appetites been too small? How might God want to expand your appetites?

e. How might this way of spirituality change what you hope for?

You may have found it hard to answer the above questions. The more difficult you found them, the more you may need to look at the depth of your relationships. Why? A person with deep relationships will have substantial insight into himself due to the feedback good relationships bring. Not only do we need deep spirituality, then, we also need vital community.

11. a. How might this group help one another to a deeper honesty and repentance about self-sufficiency?

b. How might this group help one another toward a disciple-ship that turns each appetite and desire toward heaven?

c. How might this group help one another toward a vital hope based on a deeper understanding of Isaiah 55:1-3?

12. This study is ending. Where will you go from here?

❶ *Have someone read the following essay aloud.*

Individual spirituality, important though it is, must be deepened, broadened, and sharpened by connecting deeply with other believers in committed relationships (what Scripture calls fellowship). Too often, believers have few vital, living bonds holding them together. They are more like a pile of sand than a group of living cells.[1] The sand grains are near each other but are not interconnected. *Christians are to be connected.*

Connecting, though, can be scary. We have a habit of faking connection through small talk, cliché-riddled conversation, and scripted responses to one another. These are the "fig leaves" with which we cover our nakedness. We need to get past this protectiveness. We are meant to know and be known. Scripturally, knowing another involves a deep—even costly—care and concern that results in loving action.

Assignment   5 minutes

Take out a sheet of paper and write across it the four headings from the chart on page 87. Under each heading write three prayers that you want to pray regarding the issue that column addresses (such as "honesty"). Then write three actions you want to take to apply the issues in that column to your life (such as "Here are three ways in which I want to be more honest with myself and others. ").

Prayer   5 minutes

Beginning with the leader, complete this statement for the person on your right: "One thing I have gained from you during this group is . . ." Let each person pray aloud, beginning with the leader. Thank God for what you have gained from this group, and pray together for His wisdom. If you would rather pray silently, please say "Amen" aloud to let the other people know you are finished.

Reference Notes

But while he was still a long way off: It seems that the father in the story had been watching for his son. We can't know how often he went out to scan the horizon for him, but the point is clear: this father was anxious for his son's return and was vigilantly, lovingly watching for him.

he ran: In ancient Near Eastern cultures older people were regarded with respect and accorded great dignity. Part of being dignified as an elderly one in those cultures was never to hurry oneself. The fact that this father *ran* to meet his son means that he threw off all dignity in his delight to embrace him.

robe, ring, and sandals: These were all marks of sonship. The father was saying, in effect, "No! You will never be a hired man of mine. You are my son, and I will mark you as my son in every way I can think of!"

he was lost and is found: The point of the story is here. Jesus tells His hearers that God delights in finding what is lost and goes to great, generous, gracious effort to do so.

▼ ▼ ▼ ▼ ▼ ▼ ▼ ▼ ▼ ▼ ▼ ▼ ▼ ▼ ▼ ▼ ▼ ▼ ▼ ▼

Additional Resources

Crabb, Larry. *Connecting*. Grand Rapids, Mich.: Zondervan, 1997.
Lovelace, Richard. *Dynamics of Spiritual Life*. Downers Grove, Ill.: InterVarsity, 1979.

▼ ▼ ▼ ▼ ▼ ▼ ▼ ▼ ▼ ▼ ▼ ▼ ▼ ▼ ▼ ▼ ▼ ▼ ▼ ▼

Food for Thought

"A broken and contrite heart is a formidable thing in God's hand. His Kingdom advances on the shoulders of those who refuse to be put off or satisfied with less."

—David Swartz,
Dancing with Broken Bones
(Colorado Springs, Colo.: NavPress, 1987)

---

1. Richard Lovelace, *Dynamics of Spiritual Life* (Downers Grove, Ill.: InterVarsity, 1979), p. 171.

AUTHOR

STEVE SHORES is a private practice counselor and writer in Hickory, North Carolina. Formerly, he served as assistant professor of Pastoral Ministries and director of counseling services at Dallas Theological Seminary.

If you liked Managing Stress, be sure to check out these other PILGRIMAGE studies.

Seeking God's Will

This eight-week PILGRIMAGE guide introduces readers to some of the fundamental issues around discerning God's will and examines the role of community in the decision-making process.

Seeking God's Will
(Dudley Delffs) $6.50

Living by the Spirit

By tracing the unfolding picture of the Holy Spirit in the New Testament, this nine-session study guide gives group members a clear and complete understanding of the Holy Spirit's role in their lives.

Living by the Spirit
(Marlene Nathan) $6.50

Mastering Money

This eight-week PILGRIMAGE guide will get you and your group talking about money. Together you will develop new attitudes toward money, grow in accountability, and discover how to depend on God—not money—for security, hope, and identity.

Mastering Money
(Dudley Delffs) $6.50

Get your copies today at your local bookstore, visit our website at www.navpress.com, or call (800) 366-7788 and ask for offer **#2168**.

NAVPRESS
BRINGING TRUTH TO LIFE

Prices subject to change without notice.